GENIUS ANDROID MARKETING

GET RICH BY OUTSMARTING THE ANDROID MARKET

JAY VAN BUITEN

Genius Android Marketing

By Jay Van Buiten

Portions of this book are modifications based on work created and shared by Google and used according to terms described in the Creative Commons 3.0 Attribution License.

TABLE OF CONTENTS

1 INTRO

Don't skip this

There are 200,000 apps on the Android Market. TWO HUNDRED THOUSAND. How many can you name? You, an Android developer, way more familiar with the market than the average person, can name… 100? How many have you heard about or seen on a blog or seen on TV? Maybe a thousand? So you've never even heard of or seen 99.5% of the Android apps on the market. **Almost every app fails.** You will too – if you think that developing an above-average app and uploading it to the market is all you need to do.

GENIUS TIP: Just about every app fails.

Go on the market real quick and pick any category. Now spend 10 minutes scrolling down. Just keep going. At this point, most of the apps that you'll see suck, but if you look closely, there are some that don't. There's nothing groundbreaking down there, but there's some good, useful, fun, above-average apps - and no one will ever see them.

So be honest with yourself – if you already have an app idea, is it any better than that decent app you found in the dark depths of the Android Market? It's probably a good idea, something that someone, somewhere will want to use. But is it so groundbreaking, so awesome that it can't possibly fail? It's not. So how do you avoid meeting the same fate as all those other "good ideas" that never made a dime? The answer is by being smarter than everyone else.

While the statistics don't look good, there is good news. The Android Market is fairly new – it's not like the web where an entire industry of marketing and SEO professionals spend day and night figuring out how to game the system and get to the top of the Google results. The truth is almost no one knows what they are doing. In fact, at the time of this writing, this is the first full-size book to have ever been written about Android Marketing. (There's another by Jeffery Hughes, but it's literally an iPhone book with the words changed around. I hope you didn't already waste your money like I did.) There are very few people that know how to make sure an Android app succeeds.

Since the competition is so unknowledgeable, it simply isn't very hard to successfully market your app if you know what you are doing – if you do ANY marketing at all, you've already done more than 95% of the developers out there. I've been doing Android development since the beginning, and I've learned a lot about what makes an app successful, and what makes it a failure – and most of it is not obvious information. In this book I will present everything I've learned – what I did right, and what I did horribly, horribly wrong. I make a living developing Android apps, and you can too, but only if you outwork and outsmart the competition when it comes to marketing your app.

You can get rich on your Android app – but only if you have smarter publicity, smarter design, smarter pricing, and smarter advertising than everyone else. This book will show you how.

2 MAKING YOUR APP MARKETABLE

You skipped the intro, didn't you?

If you've ever taken an introduction to marketing class, you know the single greatest asset you have when marketing is competitive advantage. A competitive advantage is something your product has that is better than the competition – a reason to buy your product as opposed to that of your competitors. The more significant your competitive advantage is, the easier it will be to convince your target audience to buy your product. When it comes to Android apps, your competitive advantage is something your app can do that no one else's can.

YOUR APP NEEDS TO BE UNIQUE.. KIND OF

The only way you're going to be able to convince your audience to buy your app is if the app has something unique about it – something they can't get on another app. This doesn't mean your app needs to do something magical and groundbreaking – you just need some way to convince people to download your app. In fact, you could even completely copy someone else's idea, having no uniqueness at all in terms of functionality, but still have a competitive advantage by making your app cheaper or better looking. For instance, a great way to find app ideas if you are looking for a new app to develop is to look for successful apps that are either overpriced or look like they were designed by a blind third grader. Just look at the Music category on the market. There are free music apps with millions of downloads that have absolutely no functionality that the *built-in* official music app doesn't have. The only advantage they have is good design. People like apps that don't hurt their eyes! But we will talk about design in a later chapter – just know that you need to have at least 1 unique selling point about your app.

GENIUS TIP: YOUR APP NEEDS AT LEAST 1 SIGNIFICANT COMPETITIVE ADVANTAGE

You can make the same app, price it cheaper, or find a sighted person to design it and make a pretty icon, and with the marketing techniques you'll learn in this book, you can take away a significant chunk of their market share. So, in conclusion, a great way to have a marketable, unique app is to copy a blind person's idea.

KEEP IT SIMPLE

I refuse to use that cringe-inducing acronym for telling stupid people to keep things simple in my book, but the same idea applies – your app needs to be simple. Think about it from a user's perspective: when you are browsing apps, or reading about a new app, or looking at a YouTube video promoting an app, how much time do you spend finding out about it before deciding whether or not to download or buy it? 30 Seconds? I could give you some newly released report about how humans spend a remarkably small amount of time making product-buying decisions, but I'm not a very good author. The point is that you need to be able to explain what is awesome about your app VERY quickly, before people stop paying attention. Your app might be great, but if you can't explain it in less time than your audience's attention span lasts, it won't sell.

GENIUS TIP: YOU SHOULD BE ABLE TO EXPLAIN YOUR APP IN 1 SENTENCE.

In addition to convincing users to buy your app, your app should also be simple and easy to explain because you're going to need to convince bloggers to write about it when you do your launch promotion and email outreach. This will be addressed more in the publicity chapter, but simplicity and a clear marketing message will help you every single step of the way in marketing your app.

It should have a simple title

The title of your app should be what the app does, period. If your app title is exactly what a user is searching for, you are basically guaranteed to appear very highly on the search results. There is no reason to have an irrelevant, hard to remember title. This isn't a hotel chain – brand loyalty doesn't mean much. Nearly all customers buy one thing from you in their lifetime, you are better off focusing all energy on making that sale instead of building a brand.

It should have a beautiful icon

Your icon should look awesome. It doesn't have to mean anything, but it should be colorful and really cool looking. It really doesn't matter if it is completely irrelevant to your app. The purpose of your icon is to catch the users eye while browsing the market and get them to read your app's title, from there, that should convince them to look at the description, which convinces them to buy your app.

You probably suck at designing things, as most developers do. Hire someone, or just use one of the thousands of free icons available on the web. Make sure you check the licensing agreements of everything before you use it.

3 HOW TO HAVE A GREAT IDEA

We'll get to a marketing chapter eventually, don't worry

Maybe you already have a great app idea and you just want to know how to market it – in that case feel free to skip this chapter and come back when you're ready to build your next app. But I feel like I have some tangible, specific tips for how to have a good idea that are not necessarily obvious, and I know a lot of people struggle, thinking "I would love to make an app but I just can't think of anything good", so I decided I'd throw that into the book as a bonus. This isn't technically a chapter about marketing, but a great app idea makes for a great app, and a great app is the easiest kind to market, so that's something, I guess. Read on if you'd like!

GENIUS TIP: IDEAS AREN'T THAT DIFFICULT

Whenever people talk to me about developing apps, I hear one assumption over and over: "Well having a good idea must be the hardest part, right?" Wrong. When it comes to apps, people assume that you just need to have that magical "great idea" and once it hits you, fame, riches and ladies just fall down on you like rain. This is false. The idea isn't hard – I have a backlog of about 20-25 good app ideas and you will too after reading this chapter and learning how to train yourself to have good app ideas. Ideas are not the hardest part of making money from Android apps

– marketing is. It took me a long time to get good at marketing and that's why I'm writing this book. But ideas aren't as magical as they sound, so here's some "secrets" to having a great idea:

CONTENT IS FREE

One of the coolest things about the internet is that so many awesome websites make their content available through extremely easy-to-use APIs, and combining content from these different sources and using the content in new ways can produce some awesome results. Just about all of my apps combine different APIs to create totally new products. I guess I'll finally mention a couple of the apps I've actually developed myself, and what APIs they use:

Ghosttown: This is my most successful app in terms of downloads (about 100,000 in the first month). It uses the Google Images API, LyricsWiki API, Billboard API, Last.fm API, and YouTube API to make basically create an infinite iPod. Users enter an artist – their discography listings are pulled from LyricWiki, album art is instantly downloaded from Google Images, songs are selected and played from YouTube, and new artists and songs are recommended thanks to last.fm and Billboard. A really awesome, unique product was developed by combining great content from a bunch of different sources.

Tablet Wallpapers: Uses the Bing API (Bing has SUCH a good API) to search for and browse tablet-sized wallpapers. A very simple app that took about 2 days to develop, it's really just a simple image-search app disguised as a wallpaper app, and it gets over 1000 active users a day and is the top ranked tablet-wallpaper app.

Number Spy: Uses 6 different APIs from various listing services and search engines, to gather information about unknown phone numbers when a call is received. Another very simple, easy to develop app that just combines a few sources of free content to do something cool.

The best place to find out about great APIs and what kind of content you can legally and freely use for your app is by browsing http://programmableweb.com on a regular basis. It's a directory and news site of APIs and mash-ups, and it's awesome. Checking this site out weekly gives me tons of simple app ideas.

GENIUS TIP: USE AWESOME, FREE CONTENT, WHICH YOU CAN FIND AT PROGRAMMABLEWEB.COM.

Another good place to hang around getting good ideas is lifehacker.com. While it is not necessarily directly related to apps, it is full of awesome tech-related ideas and making something cool out of ordinary things – which exactly what you want to do when making an app – using the tools you already have (like phone hardware, Android OS, and available content) and making something new and useful out of it.

STAY ON THE CUTTING EDGE

"All the good ideas are taken". This is something I hear from other developers all the time. Not true! Not only are there an infinite amount of good ideas left to be had (How many times a day do you see a new website or app and think "Duh! Why didn't I think of that?"), there is always an area with little to no competition: anything brand new. For instance, when Android 3.0 Honeycomb came out a few months ago, it brought a whole new API for designing apps and a whole array of Android tablets to develop for. Since I keep up with the tech blogs and android forums, I was aware of this development and was able to begin making my "Tablet Wallpapers" app the first day the API and emulator became available to developers. Consequently, my tablet wallpapers was the first one to market, and is currently the most-downloaded wallpapers app that is made specifically for tablets. This successful app didn't require a genius idea – wallpaper apps are one of the most common and competitive niches on the marketplace – it just took me staying on the cutting edge of developments of the Android OS and jumping on as soon as I got the chance. As the market share for Android tablets grow, so will the download numbers for my wallpapers app.

A brand new development in the Android world is Google Wallet NFC payment system. This allows you to use your phone as a payment system use Near Field Communication. The system is compatible with MasterCard PayPass vendors, so there are already a ton of places for NFC enabled-phones to spend money with having to carry a credit or debit card. The first people to jump on board with even the most basic and obvious NFC apps are guaranteed to get a huge amount of downloads and publicity. If you don't have an app idea right now and I'd recommend developing an NFC app – it's looking like it's going to get real big, real soon.

As long as you keep an eye on the newest developments there is a lot of market share to be had if you are willing to take the risk and jump on board.

They key is to keep up with the blogs and surround yourself with the newest ideas and you'll find yourself with a lot less competition than with old niches.

BE A COPYCAT!

Sometimes the best ideas are already taken. Doesn't mean you can't use them! Like we've discussed, there are a lot of great ideas that are buried deep in the Android Market with terrible sales numbers. There is nothing wrong with taking those great ideas, designing them better, executing them better, and marketing them better to create a successful app! In fact, they are tons of Music apps that use YouTube to let people listen to huge amounts of music, but none of them put everything together in a clean, simple, organized fashion – that's why I created Ghosttown, which recently hit 250,000 download in just a couple of months.

Sometimes there are a lot of apps in a small niche, but none of them do the job perfectly. If you see that the best app in a niche has less than 4 stars, take a shot at it! Read the reviews to see what people don't like about the existing apps, and create an app that finally gives users everything they want! In fact, "copycat" apps carry the least development risk – you already know how large the potential user base is, what your users want, and how successful you can be. Don't be afraid to copy a great app! But again – make sure there is significant room for improvement over the existing app, and know that you are capable of creating an app that is significantly better – not just in your mind, but in the mind of the users.

OPEN SOURCE!

For reasons that I do not understand, there are some very talented developers that spend a lot of time making really good apps, and then they release them for free and make them open source. This means you can use all or some of the code in making your own app, and depending on the license, you can even sell it. Ringdroid is probably the most famous example – while Ringdroid itself is the bestselling ringtone maker on the market, many spin-offs have been made by taking the Ringdroid code and adding small features. In fact, Ringtone Maker Pro has made tens of thousands of dollars by developing a prettier version of Ringdroid with a few small features added! There are even some apps which have done nothing more than changed the color scheme and made the UI slightly easier to use that have made hundreds or even thousands of dollars – all this from probably less than week's work from start to finish! And it's completely legal.

GENIUS TIP: IF YOU ARE JUST STARTING OUT, TRY MAKING AN APP BASED ON AN OPEN SOURCE APP

Enhancing and selling open source apps is a great way to get started developing Android apps because you can get something on the market, and learn the experience of finishing and uploading an app, without having to have a ton of development experience. As any developer knows, it is much easy to tweak an existing, working app than to start one from scratch, especially if you are not yet totally familiar with Java or Eclipse.

There are a few places with lists of open source Android apps, the biggest I've seen is Wikipedia: http://en.wikipedia.org/wiki/List_of_free_software_A ndroid_applications. It has a nice little table with license and API information as well. You should also look into the IO series of open source Android apps. It's amazing how many great apps are available as a starting point for you to use. Make sure you check the licenses of these apps and that you are legally allowed to do whatever you plan on doing!

While we are on the subject, open source apps are also great for individual Intents inside your app. For instance, there is no reason to waste time developing file browsers and barcode scanners from scratch to use in your app if you need the user to choose a file or scan a barcode. These 2 functions come to mind because I have used open source code to do both in my own apps, but nearly any common function of that nature is available through open source. Always do a quick Google search to see what you can find if you are writing code for a part of your app which has probably been written by someone before.

GENIUS TIP: DON'T WASTE YOUR TIME REINVENTING THE WHEEL

CHOOSE THE RIGHT CATEGORY

Hopefully by this point you have a couple of decent app ideas up your sleeve – otherwise a marketing book isn't going to do you much good. If you are deciding which of your ideas would eventually make a successful app, it's good to look at which categories and niches breed successful apps the most often. For instance, games make up 25% of the total apps in the Android Market, and 70% of downloaded apps! It is EXTREMELY hard to compete in the games category, and a lot of people simply aren't willing to pay for a game, so paid apps may be out of the question.

GENIUS TIP: GAMES ARE A VERY HIGH-RISK, HIGH-REWARD CATEGORY: HIGH COMPETITION, AND PAID APPS ARE HARD TO SELL. BUT IT'S THE ONLY CATEGORY THAT CAN MAKE YOU A MILLIONAIRE

On the other hand, tools and utilities are great categories to develop apps for because apps are generally very simple to make, as they simply accomplish a single task, people are willing to pay for apps because they enhance the functionality and value of the phone, and there is much less competition. There are some apps in the Utilities category that have made hundreds of thousands of dollars despite only working on rooted phones! If your app is unique and does a specific task to improve or enhance the functionality of the phone, it will be easy to market and will make good money without a doubt. On the other hand, a game or multimedia app may get lost in a sea of competition and people will be less willing to pay for it.

GOOD WEBSITES MAKE GREAT APPS

Another easy way to get an idea for an app is to simply make a version of a popular website that is easier to access and made specifically for phones. Take a website that doesn't yet have a good mobile version and make an app that puts the content in a simple and easy to use mobile format. As an example, there are tons of apps that lets you read PostSecret postcards or XKCD comics – 2 tremendously popular websites with no good built-in mobile site. Make sure it's legal though! Read the websites terms of service and make sure they have an RSS feed or API, don't just steal content. Also, it is frowned upon to sell these types of apps, so you should probably market this as a free app – people are rarely willing to pay for the same content they get on a free website anyway.

DON'T THINK SO BIG, BE ANTI-SOCIAL.

We all wish we were Mark Zuckerberg: 26 Years old with $20 Billion in the bank. That's why we are independent developers – we dream of finally having that perfect idea and hitting the big-time - it's not going to happen. Don't try to change the way the world works with your app – the odds of your next huge social network catching on are not in your favor

– you having a better chance of winning the lottery while getting struck by lightning.

GENIUS TIP: YOU ARE NOT, AND NEVER WILL BE, MARK ZUCKERBERG.

Every tech entrepreneur has a game-changing (according to them) social idea, but there are currently about 3-4 social networks which people actually use. The thing about social apps is that everyone needs to use them for them to work, so they naturally require great timing and a lot of luck. I can say with a lot of certainty that no one that reads this book will ever create the next big Facebook or Twitter or FourSquare. You are better off making a solid app and aiming to bring in $100,000 a year, not $100,000,000. You don't want to spend all that time developing a sweet app only to have no one use it and still be broke. But don't take this to mean your app shouldn't have social elements: Including Twitter and Facebook elements can make your app way more useful and they should definitely be incorporated if possible - we will discuss this further in later chapters – but my advice is not to try to change the world by starting your own social network. If an app requires a lot of the user's friends to also be using it in order to work correctly, it will almost certainly fail.

4 MARKET RESEARCH

You're getting there

Before you decide to start developing your app, you need to know if it realistically has a chance to succeed. If there is already an app on the market that does the same thing, and is developed by a large corporation with a huge marketing budget, your app will not succeed. It is a good idea to do market research before you start development, potentially saving you from wasting time developing an app that is doomed to fail. On the other hand, if you have already developed your app, you still will need to do market research in order to determine how to market and price your app as successfully as possible.

IDENTIFY YOUR COMPETITORS

The first step to analyzing whether or not your app can be successful is to identify your competitors. The goal of your competitive analysis is to put yourself in the position of a user and see if you can realistically put your app in a position where a) people can find it and b) people will download it as opposed to the other choices they have. If it's realistic that users can find your app and will want to download it, then it's an app you should develop!

Now is as good a time as ever to introduce the concept of Searchers and Browsers. These are essentially the 2 ways that people find and download apps from the Market.

Searchers: These people are looking to accomplish a specific task, let's say they want an app to count their calories. They search "calorie counter" and then choose which one to download based on the titles, icons, and descriptions of the apps in the search results. They may be willing to pay to accomplish their task if they need to.

Browsers: These people are not looking to accomplish a specific task, but instead are just browsing the Market looking for something to download. They may be browsing at random or looking in a specific category that interests them, like Sports. They will read the description of any app that grabs their interest with the title and icon, and then decide whether to download. Browsers are rarely willing to pay to download an app unless the description is able to convince them that this is something they really need and can't get for free.

When identifying your competitors, you should look at the Market from the perspective of both searchers and browsers. Your competitors are those apps which are contenders in the user's decision of which app to download, whether they are in a searching or a browsing situation. I'll walk you through it from the point of view of my market research for my app "Tablet Wallpapers":

If your app is simple, doing market research from a searcher's perspective is easy: Just search whatever a typical user would search when trying to accomplish the task that your app, and your competing apps, allows them to accomplish. Our goal is to find a term (or terms) that we feel we can rank highly for, and our marketing and branding will target those terms. For Tablet Wallpapers, that task is finding new wallpapers for their Android tablet. Let's identify every common search we can think of that someone might use to accomplish this – here's what I came up with: "wallpapers", "background", "tablet wallpapers", "tablet backgrounds".

The next step in your research is to search all of those terms yourself and see what comes up. Identify which apps are irrelevant (those apps that users would never download when looking to solve your task), which apps a user could potentially download instead of yours.

"wallpapers" and "backgrounds" – All of the results were for phone background apps, and all of the top results had over a million downloads. Because the total market size for tablet users is lower than that of phone users, I decided I would never get the high amount of downloads needed to rank up there with these apps. My only hope for people using these terms was that they would see that all of the results were for phone backgrounds, not tablets, and do another search for "tablet wallpapers" or "tablet backgrounds".

"tablet wallpapers" and "tablet backgrounds" – these were the most important terms because I figured they would be the most common. After doing the search, I was pleasantly surprised to see that I couldn't find a wallpapers app made specifically for tablets! The highest ranking app was "HD Wallpapers", which is made for phones but works with tablets, and then there were a bunch of irrelevant results like live wallpaper apps and celebrity wallpaper apps. There was absolutely an untapped market for my Tablet Wallpaper app, and I determined that it was realistic that I could get myself as high as #2 in the rankings for these terms, and when presented which the choice of which app to download, people would choose mine because the title of my app tells the user that I will

36

solve their problem as opposed to "HD Wallpapers", which is a little more ambiguous. These were the terms I was going to target. Remember to put yourself in the position of the user and try to decide which app a user would pick when searching that term. If your app is paid and there is a comparable free app with decent a decent rating, they aren't going to pick yours. If you are in this situation, read the reviews for the free app. If there are a lot of people dissatisfied with free app or a lot of people complaining that it doesn't work or constantly force closes, you can still succeed.

If you can't find a term that you feel you can realistically rank highly for, don't develop your app, because users will never find you. It's as simple as that. "But what about people just browsing the market?" you may ask. People will only find your app via browsing if you are ranked highly in category rankings, and you can only do that if you already have a lot of downloads. Targeting a search term is the way you initially build your ranking in order to get those browsing downloads.

GENIUS TIP: IF YOU CAN'T REALISTICALLY TARGET A SEARCH TERM, AND YOUR APP IS NOT AN ORIGINAL IDEA, DON'T DEVELOP IT

Although there is an exception! There is always one term for which you will most likely rank highly – the name of your app. People will search for the name of your app if they have heard about your app through the blogs, Twitter, Facebook, word of mouth, etc. With successful launch marketing (which we will talk about later in the more interesting parts of this book), people will look for your app, which will build your downloads and begin to climb the rankings which will kick start those browsing downloads. But if your app is a copycat app or just improving on old ideas, blogs are unlikely to write about it and people will be less likely to tell their friends about it. To summarize: Your app either needs to be able to target a search term, or be an original idea such that blog marketing and word of mouth will be enough to succeed.

GENIUS TIP: LAUNCH MARKETING IS MUCH HARDER FOR UNORIGINAL APPS

One of the most frustrating things for most app developers is that it seems impossible to get a high ranking on the Android Market because rankings are largely based on having lots of downloads, and having lots of downloads is largely based on high rankings. But since by the end of the book you will know how to outsmart the competition when it comes to marketing, that "viscous cycle" will be an "awesome cycle", because your app will be stuck in it. The first (and one of the most important) step to breaking your app into the awesome cycle is targeting search terms because it is the only way to get downloads without being ranked highly.

GENIUS TIP: BREAK INTO THE CYCLE OF HIGH DOWNLOADS AND HIGH RANKINGS BY REALISTICALLY TARGETING 1 SEARCH TERM, EVEN IF IT'S JUST YOUR APP NAME

SALES PROJECTIONS

Let's figure out how many sales your app will get! This is the last step before we can make a final determination of whether or not your app is feasible and whether you should pull the trigger and spend the time developing. Put your app in one of three categories: Free with rare usage (apps which accomplish a task, such as my wallpaper app), Free with frequent usage (apps which users use regularly, like a music or messaging app), and Paid apps. Let's look at all 3:

Free with rare usage: these are tough to make money off of. You are going to need a huge number of downloads in order to generate the ad revenue needed to make any significant amount of money. My recommendation is to only use these types of apps as "loss leader" apps, basically apps which you only use to advertise your own paid apps. I'll go into mind-numbing detail about these types of apps in the monetization section. I have used these types of apps and had a great deal of success. If you don't have any paid apps and don't plan to, I'd recommend against creating a Free with rare usage app, it's just not realistic that you'll make a lot of money.

GENIUS TIP: ONLY DEVELOP A FREE, RARELY USED APP IF YOU PLAN TO USE IT TO ADVERTISE YOUR OTHER, PAID, APPS

Free with frequent usage: It is entirely realistic to make money on these types of apps. My music app, Ghosttown, has about 250,000 downloads as of right now and makes $80-100 a day on advertising. It's not making hundreds of thousands, but $30,000/year or so isn't bad money to be making while you sleep. It was absolutely worth it to develop the app (it took about 3 months to develop). While I don't have millions of downloads like other free apps, the fact that it is a music app which users use on a daily basis keeps my ad revenue high compared to rarely used utility apps.

Paid: It's very easy to determine how many downloads you need to make it worth it: Decide how much money you want to make, and divide by the price of the app. And don't forget that Google takes 30% of your money.

Now that you have a rough estimate in your head of how many downloads you want in order to make it worth it to develop your app, let's estimate how many downloads you'll get and then determine whether to go for it!

Can your app succeed?

Take all your competitors from your competitive analysis and take the top-ranking app that is a) the same price or more expensive than yours b) not as good an app as yours. See how many downloads it has, and how long it's been on the market (You can see the original release date on app directories like appbrain.com). This app is probably the worst-case scenario for you. Since your app is both cheaper (or the same) and better, and since you'll have a smarter marketing plan because you've read this book, you will be able to beat this app. If the app in question makes a decent amount of money, then go ahead and develop yours because you'll make more (As long as you finish reading the book!)

Hopefully you were able to determine that it is worth the time to make your app. If so, keep reading! The book is about to get more interesting, as I show you how to make the most money possible with your app, and give you quite a few tips and secrets on Android Marketing that you won't find anywhere else.

5 PRICING

Decisions, decisions

Finally! We have reached a chapter that people care about. The single biggest decision you'll make while marketing your app (although I'll probably say that a few more times): How much will it cost? When users decide whether to download your app, they are weighing the value they will get out of the app versus the value of the money and time they give up. Deciding how much money users will need to give up will have a huge effect on your number of downloads, and consequently how much money you will make. It's not an easy decision, and it could mean the difference between making a living on your apps and getting a real job. Don't mess it up! Luckily for you, I've been through this decision a number of times, made some mistakes, and now can communicate to you how to make the right decision. Let's start with the most important, easiest to remember genius tip in the entire book:

GENIUS TIP: DO NOT, UNDER ANY CIRCUMSTANCES, PRICE YOUR APP AT $0.99

We are going to discuss the scenarios in which you should release your app for free, which ones should be free with a pro version, which ones should make money on in-app billing, which ones should cost a couple bucks, and which should be higher-cost premium apps, but the important thing to remember is that no app should ever be priced at $0.99. Ever. Here's why:

You can usually double your income by charging $1.99 instead: In my own experience, and from reading studies and talking to other developers, users are just as likely to pay for an app at $1.99 or $2.99 as they are at $0.99. In other words, very few people that ARE willing to pay $0.99 AREN'T willing to pay $1.99. For just about everyone, if they are willing to pay for something, they are willing to pay at least $3. There's a peak on the curve somewhere, but it's almost always higher than $0.99.

People give more bad reviews at $0.99: The more value (money) that a user gives up for an app, the more that user will want to like the app, justifying the purchase in his or her mind. When you buy an expensive gadget, don't you try hard to convince yourself you made the right decision by focusing on the good features and ignoring the bad ones? The same goes for apps. At higher price points, users are more likely to take the time and learn to use the app, because they want to like it. At $0.99, they are more likely to dismiss it if they have a bad first impression and leave a bad review.

You miss out on free publicity: There are a number of websites which monitor the Android Market and will automatically report when an app drops their price. When a popular app offers a discount, it generates some buzz around the blogosphere (yea, I said it) and Twitter. If your app is already at the Android minimum of $0.99, it's impossible to offer discount, missing out on free publicity.

GENIUS TIP: TEMPORARY PRICE DROPS GENERATE FREE AND AUTOMATIC PUBLICITY

You'll get a higher ranking at higher prices: For the same reason you'll get better reviews at a higher price, you'll also have a higher ranking because your retention rate will be higher. Retention rate (also called active user rate) is the percentage of users who have still have your app installed out of the total number of downloads. Google uses it as a measure of user satisfaction along with the ratings system. The more a user pays for an app, the more hesitant they will be to uninstall it, even if they don't use it.

While there are situations and justifications for just about any other price point, there is no reason to price your app at $0.99. When compared to a higher price, you'll make less money, get worse reviews, and miss out on free publicity.

Now that I've hopefully convinced you NOT to price your app at $0.99, you still need to decide between every other possibility. In the rest of this section, we'll talk about basing your price on your competitive research, using your price as your competitive advantage, and talk about the pros and cons of both free and paid apps.

Base your price on market research

While the price of your app is based on quite a few factors such as the category, uniqueness, and whether or not you will use it to promote other apps, the single biggest factor to consider when deciding on a price for your app is the price of the competition. If your app is both less valuable and more expensive than the competition, your app won't succeed. You once again need to put yourself in the position of both searches and browsers and decide which price will be most effective in striking a balance between pricing the app low enough to convince users to download your app instead of the competition, while on the other hand pricing it high enough that you can meet your revenue goals.

First, do a search for your targeted search term, and consider the following questions:

Which other apps might the user choose to download instead of mine?

Maybe you have a unique app and they are no other apps that do what yours do. In this case, you should charge for your app. A unique app that adds functional value to a phone with no legitimate alternatives can be successful by charging a higher price ($2.99-$4.99). If your app is unique but is more of an entertainment app, such as a music app or a game, you should still consider making it a free app as paid entertainment apps are much harder to market. If you have a unique app, you can be successful either way and you can make that decision as we go more in depth into the ups and downs of both free and paid apps later in the chapter.

On the other hand, your app probably has some competition, and in most cases your app will have quite a bit of competition. In this case, the answer is a lot less clear, and picking the wrong price could mean the difference between meeting your revenue goals and failing. Hopefully, you read the sections about app ideas and competitive advantage before developing your app, so your app has more value to users than your competitors. If so, you should be able to charge for your app, somewhere in the $1.99-$2.99 range. If there are a variety of good, well designed free apps on the market that are competing with yours, you should consider making your app free. If your app is free AND has competitive advantage in a niche with a large market size (games, music, entertainment, utilities, etc), you can still make enough money with ad revenue to meet your goals with a well-marketed app.

Are my paid app competitors selling as well as I want to sell?

If your paid competitors are not making anywhere near as much money as you hope to make, you should try to find out why – investigate the following possibilities:

Does it have a bad rating? Maybe users are not satisfied. Users rarely read reviews of free apps, but you can be sure they will read at least the first few reviews before forking over their credit card number.

A few bad ratings can kill sales. In fact, I have seen my own sales drop over 80% when I have a bad rating and bad recent reviews when compared to when I have a good rating and my last 3 reviews were 4+ stars.

Was it poorly marketed? Do a quick Google search and try to see if the app was ever featured on any well-known android blogs. Also check out twitter to see if anyone talks about it. If not, the low sales could be due to the fact that the developer did no marketing whatsoever.

Is it brand new? Maybe you were surprised to see a seemingly good app has less than 100 all-time downloads, but you should check appbrain.com to make sure the app didn't just get released this week. In fact, AppBrain will tell you the dates the app was released, along with the dates that the app hit each download milestone, so you can estimate exactly how many downloads it has at the moment, divide by the number of days since it's been released, multiply by 365, and see how much they make per year.

GENIUS TIP: USE APPBRAIN TO EASILY ESTIMATE A COMPETITORS YEARLY REVENUE

If checking out any of these possibilities brought an obvious answer as to why a competitor doesn't have many downloads, it may still be feasible for you to charge for your app, assuming you can avoid the same problems. If the app turns out to have been well marketed, gets good reviews by those who do download it, and it's been around for a while, you may just need to face the facts and realize there is not a very large group of people who are willing to pay for your type of app.

Price can be your competitive advantage if needed

If you chose to go the route of developing a copycat app, you should at least have an app that is designed and marketed a lot better than the app whose functionality you copied. If you still don't feel like you have added enough value to your app to make it a clearly superior alternative to the app you copied, don't worry, because you can still be successful – price can be your competitive advantage. Like we discussed, users don't see a lot of difference between apps priced between $0.99 and $2.99, so if the competitor's app is priced in that range, you should strongly consider making your app free. If the competitor is priced at $3.99+, you can provide an advantage on price by pricing your app at $1.99 or $2.99. Lastly, if the competitor's app is free, and you don't feel like your app has enough added value on better design and marketing alone, than you shouldn't have developed your app in the first place. Open up Eclipse and figure out a way to add a significant feature that your competitor doesn't have, and make sure your app is much easier, faster, and more pleasant to use than your competitor.

Paid Apps: Things to consider

Set a realistic goal, and work towards it.

If you have a specific financial goal you are trying to reach, it's a good idea to see how many sales you need in order to meet the goal, and then decide if that's realistic. For a $2.99 (which is the price I'd recommend for most paid apps, we'll discuss that more in detail later) app, you'll make $2.09 per sale. If your goal is to make $50,000 per year, you'll need to make $137 per day, which is about 66 sales per day. So if you can sell an app every 20 minutes, you'll be making more than $50,000 a year. It's easy to see why marketing is so important: If you can break your app into the top rankings in your category, it is not at all unrealistic that you could make $50,000-$100,000 a year while you sleep. If your competitive research indicates that similar apps are making this kind of money, you can probably make even more since you will have a better marketing strategy.

GENIUS TIP: SELLING A $3 APP EVERY 20 MINUTES WILL NET OVER $50K/YEAR.

While other experts may disagree, I think it's a good idea to have a realistic goal for how much revenue you expect to take in with your app. Some may say that setting a goal is putting an unnecessary ceiling on your possibilities, but I think setting a realistic goal based on your competitive research of how much money you could make if you developed and marketed your app as well as possible can be very helpful and gives you something to work towards. If you are nowhere near your daily revenue goal after a few weeks, you know you have more work to do and you must be doing something wrong or missing a key area in your marketing plan, as long as you know your original goal was realistic.

You're not going to be a multi-millionaire

We've all heard the stories of the app developer (probably an iPhone developer) who spend a week making an app, and got lucky and hit it big on the app store, and is now a millionaire at 20 years old. Maybe that's even the reason you started making apps in the first place – personally, I read the story of a app store millionaire and immediately downloaded the Android SDK and got to work on the first app I thought of. But it's important to understand how rare those situations are. They are very rare on the iPhone platform, and they quite frankly don't really happen on the Android platform. Much less money (less than $1/10^{th}$!) is spent on the Android Market than the app store, and the Market just isn't set up for one app to make hundreds of thousands a month like the App Store is. While there are very, very few apps making $1,000,000 a year, they are tons that make $50,000-$200,000, and you don't even have to get lucky to do it. If your competitive research was done right, and you have an app that people are willing to pay for, and willing to choose to download over its competitors, you can absolutely make a very good living from a well-marketed and well-maintained app. Starting in the next chapter (Publicity), I'll show you how to make sure people see your app and you get the download numbers you are looking for.

Paid apps make traditional marketing more difficult

The most important, and most effective way to get the word out about your app when launching it is by getting popular android and tech blogs to write about it. In order to convince a blogger to write about your app, they need to get something out of it. The reason bloggers like to write about new apps is because they are getting free content for their blog and providing their readers with information they want to hear – but that's the important part – it needs to be something that their readers want to hear. If your app is a paid app, the blog entry will sound more like they are trying to sell something, and less like they are trying to let their readers know about an awesome app. Blogs are much more likely to write about apps which are free so they can provide a direct download link to the market and satisfy their readers by providing them with an app without the readers needing to give anything in return. This is not to say that it is impossible to market a paid app – there are plenty of blogs which are totally willing to write about paid apps – it just needs to be a little more unique, a little more groundbreaking. If the app is worth paying for, then the blog is still providing valuable information to the reader by letting them know about it. If your app is the same old type of app as something that's already on the market, blogs are not going to be as willing to write about it, and your launch marketing will suffer.

Paid apps make social and viral marketing more difficult

This one is a little more obvious. If you are trying to market a free app, you can use buttons inside of your app to let users share direct download links to their friends through Twitter, Facebook, SMS, etc. If your app is paid, users will not only be a lot less likely to want to tell their friends about it, but you also would need to provide a link to the market page instead of a direct download link. In addition to in-app buttons to allow users to spread the word, users are also much less likely to talk about your app in person to their friends, or talk about it on social networks. If they don't feel like they could convince their friends to spend money on the app, they probably won't bring it up in the first place. With a free app, word of mouth can spread like wildfire as direct download links are easily shared and people can't wait to tell their friends about it – especially for an app with a social component, where having friends join provides value to the original user.

Users are much less willing to pay for apps on Android when compared to iPhone

The most shocking and most disappointing statistic for Android developers is that despite the fact the number of Android phones sold has surpassed the number of iPhones sold, the amount of money spent on the iOS app store is still higher. How much higher? You might not want to keep reading because the answer is depressing: The iOS App Store had more than $1.7 Billion in revenue in 2010. The Android Market? $100 Million. That's right – despite the fact that there are actually more Android users than iPhone users, iPhone users spend 17 times more money. Now before you throw this book in the garbage and buy that copy "iOS Development for Dummies" from Amazon, you should know that even though that marketing on iPhone is tougher: there is much more competition in that there are many times more quality apps, and many more of them are professionally developed and well marketed. Also, because the iOS environment is much, much more restrictive in terms of what you can do (No access to the file system, no access to undocumented methods, apps rejected for inconsistent design, etc), there are a lot less possibilities when it comes to which apps you can develop. This means you have a lot more quality apps and less variety of apps, which means a lot more competition and a lot less chance that users will stumble upon your app in the app store.

An important thing to remember when setting a price on your app is to never, ever think you can duplicate the success of an iPhone app, or assume that people are willing to pay for your app just because iPhone users are willing to pay for a similar app on the App Store. The App Store and the Android Market are two entirely different worlds, and sales numbers, competitive analysis, and market research absolutely do not translate. If you heard about some kid who made $2 Million by making a nice little app for the iPhone, don't think you put out a clone on Android and make the same money. Android users are not nearly as willing to pay for apps. Again, this is not a reason to release a great app with a huge competitive advantage for free – paid apps can still be successful. If you have an app and your competitive research indicates that your target market is willing to pay for it, then go ahead and make it a paid app.

People are more willing to write bad reviews on paid apps

As I've said throughout this book, if you have a great app charge for it. But let's take a look at the other side of the coin: If you don't have a great app, and you charge for it, you will pay the price. As we know, Android users don't like to pay for apps, and when they do, they expect a lot. With Google's recent change to the app refund policy, changing the automatic refund option from 24 hours to 15 minutes, users will not be happy if the app is buggy or doesn't do what they expect it to do. If they discover that the app frequently force closes and they are already past the 15-minute refund window, they will be upset and they will not hesitate to voice that displeasure via a 1-star review. On the other hand, for a free app, users are more willing to simply uninstall the app and cut their losses. While there are always users itching to give their opinion on a public forum for any type of app, users will be more angry about a buggy paid app than a free one, and that will be reflected in the app reviews, which will negatively affect your Market ranking and sales.

Situations when your app should be paid

Choosing between selling your app and giving it away for free in order to make money on ads or in-app purchases is not an easy decision, but they are some situations when you should be more inclined to make your app paid. While being in just one of these situations is not always a reason to go for a paid app, if you find yourself in more than one of these scenarios you should seriously consider charging for your app:

- **You have a significant competitive advantage**

  If you can honestly say you offer something to users that they can't get anywhere else, don't be afraid to charge money for your app. But keep in mind that your competitive advantage should be significant. If there is some function that your apps serves that simply isn't available anywhere else on the market, go ahead and charge for it. On the other hand, if your advantage is simply better design and an easier interface, and the competitive is full of free apps, people are probably not willing to pay just for an ease-of-use upgrade, unless of course you fit in one or more of the remaining scenarios.

- **Your app adds functionality to the user's phone**

  There are some apps that add value to a phone – they allow the user to do something with their phone that they couldn't do before. For instance, a flashlight app adds value to the phone: it is now no longer a phone, but it is also a flashlight. On the other hand, I wouldn't consider a music app like Pandora to be something that adds value to the phone. You could always listen to music on your phone, this is just a different, perhaps better, way to do it. If you app adds a function, as opposed simply improving upon a function, users are more willing to pay for it. I'll give another example: You can pretty much set any image as your wallpaper with a stock phone by just search the web, saving any image, and setting it as a wallpaper. Wallpaper apps make this process much simpler, but they don't really add functionality to the phone. For this reason, people are not willing to pay for the app, but they certainly gobble up free wallpaper apps like it's free candy. If your app streamlines a phone's functionality as opposed to adding to it, you should seriously consider making it a free app.

- **You are dealing with a money-spending audience**

  Here's something we haven't covered at all yet in the book. You need to think about the type of audience you are marketing to. If you are going to be marketing your app to an audience that has shown they are willing to spend money, then don't be a afraid to charge for your app. There is basically just 1 app priced over $9.99 that has had any significant success, and it's "Golfshot Golf GPS", priced at $29.99! The people behind Golfshot understand their audience: Golf is an expensive hobby, and golfers are clearly willing to spend quite a bit of money on their hobby. While charging 30 bucks for an app seems ridiculous to a lot of app developers, something that can significantly improve a golfer's game for just a fraction of the cost of 1 day at the course? It almost sounds a like a bargain! If you are marketing to people who have already shown a willingness to pay for their hobby, go ahead and charge for it – in fact, don't be afraid to charge a lot.
- **You app saves or makes people money**

This one is pretty obvious: If your app allows users to make money or save money, they will be more willing to pay for it because they will be able to make the money back and hopefully a lot more. For instance, I used to have a craigslist app that allowed users to search all of Craigslist (as opposed to individual cities) for items they were looking for. By being able to look at all of Craigslist, users could save a lot of money over searching on regular stores like Amazon or just 1 Craigslist city. Of course, you still need to have that competitive advantage in order to charge for an app. Had there been a free app which allowed users to do the same thing, nobody would've paid for the app.

How much should you charge?

If you've decided to charge for your app, the next decision you need to make in your marketing plan is exactly how much you are going to charge. If you are listening to what I am trying to say at all, you have already made the decision to not charge $0.99. But they are a lot of other possibilities to consider, and making the right decision will have an enormous effect on how much money you will make selling your app. At $0.99, you'll sell more apps but make only $0.69 each sale. On the other hand, charging $99.99 nets you $69.99 per sale, but then again, at that price you'll most likely sell exactly zero. Somewhere in between there is a peak at which you will make the maximum amount of money, and your job is to find it as soon as possible. Here's a few points to consider:

The competition

If you have paid apps as competition, you either need to provide more value than they do, or charge less than they do – it's that simple. If there are no apps that do what yours does, and your app is not aimed at a "premium" audience like Golfshot, I recommend shooting for the $2.99-$4.99 range. Not many users will give up on the only option for accomplishing a task over 3 bucks. Charging less than $2.99 causes you to miss out on a lot of money – for instance, you simply are not going to lose 50% of your customers by charging 50% more than $1.99. Disregarding competition, the peak for a paid app is always at least $2.99. If you have paid competition, it may be a different story. If you have better design, icon, titles, and ease-of-use than your competition, you could charge the same price as your competitor, but I would hesitate before charging more than that unless you have a functional advantage.

Audience

Consider your audience before setting your price. While most apps don't have the sort of target market than you can pin down as "high-spenders" or "cheapskates", there are some apps that you can feel comfortable charging more for, or hesitate to set a high price for, because of the audience. For instance, an app like Golfshot aimed an obviously high-spending audience can be set above a few dollars without potential buyers scoffing at the price. On the other hand, an app aimed at an age group that has smartphones but typically don't have credit cards, like younger teens, probably won't sell very well as a paid app. If you are planning on developing the next big Justin Bieber fan app, aimed at 12 year old girls, you should probably investigate an ad-based revenue model. While most typical apps, such as a Music app or a Utility app, or even a game have such a wide audience that it's impossible to classify it as a spending or non-spending audience, there are some apps where the target market should dictate the price, so make sure you are thinking about this while developing your app.

Reviews

Perhaps an effect of higher or lower pricing that is less frequently discussed is the effect that pricing has on reviews. Higher priced apps will sell at a lower volume, so you will have your app reviewed less frequently. This means that each individual review is much more important as it will stay on the front page of your app listing on the Android Market much longer. It is not uncommon for an app priced at $4.99, selling less than 20 or 30 copies a day, to have less than 4-5 reviews a week. If someone has trouble using your app and gives it a one-star rating, it may have a seriously negative effect on your sales for days at a time as users see it immediately after clicking on your app listing. On the other hand, an app making the same amount of money, priced at $0.99 but selling 150 apps a day, may have a 1-star review stay on the front screen of the listing for less than 1 day. No matter how good your app is, there are going to be dumb people who can't figure out how to use it, or didn't read the app description, that give your app one star. Be prepared for the fact that with a higher priced app, individual reviews will have a much higher impact on daily sales.

Launch pricing

As we will discuss in excruciating detail in the next chapter, the first week of sales for your app is immensely important. During the first week, you want to sell as many apps as possible to increase your sales acceleration, one of the largest factors in determining your ranking on the Android Market listings.

GENIUS TIP: ACCELERATION OF SALES MAY BE THE LARGEST FACTOR IN MARKET RANKINGS

Having a huge first week will also land you on the new "Trending Apps" list in the Market. Being ranked highly on these lists will have an enormous effect on your long-term sales, so during the first week after launch, your sales volume is actually more important than your revenue. For this reason, you may want to introduce special launch pricing. Price your app at $1.99 or so, even if you plan on your long term pricing being $3-$5.

GENIUS TIP: SALES VOLUME IS MORE IMPORTANT THAN REVENUE DURING YOUR FIRST WEEK

Also make sure you mention the sale in your app description so users know they need to buy now or they might regret it. So even if you've read this chapter and decided on a good price, you may want to go low for the first week or so, then boost the price to what you decided on.

Free Apps: Things to consider

Free apps are easier to market

Quite simply, free apps are way easier to market. Blogs are much more willing to write about free apps as that kind of content is much more valuable to their readers. Also, while viral marketing is almost a non-factor on paid apps, free apps can spread like wildfire. Users can easily provide each other with links to download the app directly, and friends will be willing to take a shot at using the app based on a friend's recommendation even if they aren't sure they will like it, because there's no risk if you don't need to pay. Essentially, paid apps need to rely a lot more on good search rankings within the Market, while free apps can get by on good marketing and word-of-mouth without being the most visible apps on the Market.

Your app should have a wide audience

Of course, there are 2 traditional ways to make money on a free app – ads and in-app purchases. We will treat in-app purchases as a separate type of app and discuss it in the next section, so that leaves us with ads. While there other, less tangible ways to make money on free apps which will be addressed in the monetization section, if you are going to release your app for free, you need to be making money on ads. In order to do that, you need to sell A LOT of copies of your app. To give you an idea of what we are looking at in terms of numbers, here are my ad revenue stats from my free app Ghosttown:

Downloads: 240,000

Average sessions per day: 40,000

Average ad impressions per day: 300,000

Average ad revenue per day: $90

I make in the neighborhood of $90 per day despite getting over 9,000 downloads per day. In order to make the same money with a paid app priced at $2.99, I'd need just 40-45 downloads. The bottom line is you need seriously large numbers of downloads to make a lot of money on a free app. If you are going to give away your app for free, make sure your competitive analysis indicates that our app can get in the range of 250,000-1,000,000 downloads in the first few months. If your app is targeted at a small audience, you should probably make it a paid app. In the case of Ghosttown, being a music app it has an incredible amount of competition and my competitive analysis indicated that users simply weren't willing to pay for a music app. Luckily my potential audience was very large and similar apps were posting download numbers in the millions, so it was a perfect app to release for free.

It should be a frequently used app

Ad money is made when users click on ads. The more ad "impressions" (every time a new ad is shown to the user counts as an impression) that are shown to the user, the more clicks you will get. A simple utility app that is used for 10 seconds at a time and only used once a month is never going to make a lot of ad revenue despite huge amounts of downloads because there just isn't much opportunity for users to click on ads. On the other hand, an app that engages the user (and keeps them engaged) has a chance to make a significant amount of money on ads without an astronomical amount of downloads because so many more ads will be shown to each user. News aggregator apps (like Pulse or an RSS reader) are great aps to show ads on for two reasons: 1. These apps keep users engaged for a long period of time, allowing you to show more ad impressions per download. 2. The large amount of text on these apps provide a lot of meta data content to the ad provider, allowing them to show relevant ads to the user, meaning the user has a larger chance of being interested in the ad, and that will increase your click-through rate. Music or video apps also are great apps because they are used for extended periods of time. When deciding whether to monetize your app with ads, remember that it's not about the number of downloads that determines your ad revenue, it's (**Number of downloads * Usage time per user * Click-through rate**). Great marketing can get you a lot of downloads, but the nature of your app is just as important: Will users use your app long enough to notice your ads? Is there content in your app which allows you to provide metadata to ad providers and show relevant ads?

You app should a have logical space for ads

Where your ads are placed on your app can have an extremely large impact on your click-through rate, which, in turn, has a large impact on your revenue. Design ads into your layout when designing your app – ad placement should not be an afterthought! If an ad looks like it fits right in the layout, instead of being an eyesore which kills the good design of your app, users will be more likely to spend that ½ second reading the ad and deciding whether or not to click it. If you can't find a way to incorporate traditional banner ads into your app, consider alternatives like video or audio ads, or even consider making an individual deal with a sponsor to integrate ads into your content instead of using an ad network.

Video ads make way more money

Video ads make a LOT more money than traditional banner ads. Typical revenue numbers for Android banner ads run from about $0.25-$1.00 eCPM. This means for every 1000 ads shown to your users, you make between $0.25-$1.00. On the other hand, 15 or 30 second full-screen video ads can make between $5-$15 eCPM. Of course, you can't show a video ad before every single activity on your app like you can with a banner ad, and users hate video ads in most situations – you can't just put video ads on a news or utility app.

GENIUS TIP: VIDEO ADS MAKE A LOT OF MONEY, BUT BE CAREFUL NOT TO ANNOY YOUR USERS

Users simply will not tolerate waiting to view content that they can get somewhere else right now. I would only recommend video ad in two situations: First, an app which shows videos to users may want to show a 15 second ad to a user once per session or so. Showing an ad every single time will result in some poor Market reviews, but the occasional ad may be tolerated based on your target market. Second, the best circumstance in which to show a video ad is somewhere where they need to wait anyway. For instance, consider an app which converts videos between different file types. The user may need to wait 30-45 seconds while the video converts anyway, so why not show a video ad at the same time as your conversion progress bar? As long as you can demonstrate to the user that you are not wasting any more of their time than they need to spend anyway, video ads are much more likely to be tolerated. If you happen to have an app which allows for natural placement of video ads, strongly consider releasing your app for free, because you have a lot more potential to make money from ads than with traditional banner or text ads.

You can't change your mind

Remember, while Google allows you to change the price of paid apps as often as you'd like, you can't switch back and forth between a free and a paid app. If you decide to release your app for free, you can't choose to charge for it later, without starting over. This is why it is extremely important to consider all of the factors of paid and free apps and create a winning strategy before you launch. It is very tempting to finish coding your app and immediately throw your app up on store at whatever price first comes to mind, but the pricing of your app is the decision that will have the single greatest impact on the amount of money you will make from your app, and you should do all the research and consider all of the possibilities before making your decision.

You can make money by advertising your other apps

This is one of the reasons I wrote this book. This is a monetization strategy that is SEVERELY overlooked when you read other resources regarding Android marketing. When you release a free app with a large target audience and a great marketing strategy, you will see a significant number of downloads and you will have a huge user base. Take my app Ghosttown for example. In the first month, Ghosttown had 150,000 downloads and around 90,000 active users. I had 90,000 people that I could communicate anything I wanted to! A large user base is of immense value whether or not you actually make a lot of money on the popular app itself. Now that I had 90,000 users which would see anything I wanted to say, I decided to build a fairly generic paid app and advertise it to my Ghosttown user base. I built an app called Number Spy which researches unknown numbers and presents as much data as much possible from Google, phone book listings, telemarketer databases, etc and present it to the user so they can decide whether or not to pick up the call. There are other apps that do similar things and I would not have made this app if I didn't have the Ghosttown user base because my competitive analysis indicated that competition was too high and I did not have much of a competitive advantage over similar apps. When I first released Number Spy it made a very paltry income of $6-$12 a day. Then I decided to start leveraging my Ghosttown user base to help sell Number Spy. I made an ad for Number Spy which fit well in the layout of the first activity of Ghosttown and set it up to display automatically on the bottom of the screen to every American user of Number Spy (Number Spy is only available in the U.S. since it only has access to U.S. phone listings). My revenue for Number Spy shot up to $50-$60 a day! I was making approximately an extra $16,000 a year due to leveraging the user base of my free app. In fact, the additional revenue for

Number Spy was nearly as significant as the traditional ad revenue from my banner ads.

If you have a great idea for an app, but your research indicates it can only be successful as a free app, and you also have an idea for a paid app that may be plagued by too much competition, consider using them in tandem to make a ton of money on 2 apps that wouldn't be successful otherwise!

In-app billing: Not as awesome as it sounds

In-app billing sounds like an awesome way to blend the attractiveness, huge downloads, and easy marketability of a free app, while still maintaining the potential to make big money. The fact is that in-app billing isn't all it's made out to be. Some of the highest-grossing apps do make their money through in-app billing, but if you look, you'll notice that all of these apps are games. IAP works well for games, and we will look into that in a bit. For now, let's discuss the pros and cons of IAP for regular apps (non-games). Unfortunately, it's mostly cons:

IAP apps are prone to lower ratings

Using an IAP app as opposed to separate free and pro versions presents one immediate disadvantage: You miss out on having a highly reviewed pro app as a result of weeding out all the bad reviews. When you have a free app and a pro app, people will try the free app, and those that love it buy the pro app. So, the only people buying and reviewing the pro app are people who will review it highly. This allows you to have a high ranking on the "pro" app section (which is actually shown before the free app section on the market) and therefore have more publicity. With IAP, any user that has a problem with the app can ruin the review score for everything, plus your app will only be listed in one section. Quite simply, IAP apps are harder to market than free/pro combinations.

GENIUS TIP: IAP APPS ARE HARDER TO MARKET TO "BROWSERS"

People are unfamiliar with IAP

This becomes less of an issue every day, but people still aren't used to in-app billing, especially on Android. With uncertainty comes less buyer confidence, which brings less sales. People aren't going to put their credit card number on something they don't recognize. While most people have confidence buying something on the Android Market because it's Google branded and trusted, people are less likely to buy something through an app made by an unknown developer. Despite the fact that it is actually the same system and just as secure, buyers don't know this.

Implementing In-app billing is really annoying

Based on my own experience, you should plan on it taking at least one day of development to implement in-app billing. It's incredibly overcomplicated and very cumbersome to test. I simply took the example app provided by Google and changed the ID of my product, and it still took several hours to get it working. Now, this shouldn't be a reason to change strategy if you have decided on IAP, but it's something I was surprised by, and something you should be aware of.

In-app billing is buggy

This is something that is entirely unacceptable and hopefully will be fixed very soon. I have looked at my error reports and seen multiple errors per week coming from files in the in-app billing library that I haven't even edited. When I implemented in-app billing (to provide the option to remove ads on

Ghosttown), I simply took the example implementation and changed ID of the sample product to my product, and yet I saw FC errors coming from unedited Google produced files. Having people run into FC errors that I didn't cause WHILE they are trying to send me money is simply unacceptable.

IAP to remove ads doesn't make much money

I can speak directly from experience on this one also. Ghosttown was getting 5,000 downloads a day, with ads on every screen of the app. On the first screen (a listview menu), I advertised a clear option to remove ads for just $0.99. Even if just 1% of users opted to remove ads, I would make $50/day, that's nearly $20,000 a year on top of my ad revenue! Unfortunately, I didn't get anywhere near 1%. Meanwhile, about a year back I had a craigslist app with a similar revenue model, except I set it up with a pro version and a free version. Here's the stats for each:

Ghosttown with IAP: 5,000 downloads a day, about 20 IAP purchases per day to remove ads

Craigslist Elite Free / Craiglist Elite: 500 Downloads a day, about 50 purchases of pro version @ $1.99

Both were simply offering ad-free version as a paid upgrade, but Craigslist, with its separate pro version, got more exposure via the Market with its listing on the paid category, didn't suffer from buyer uncertainty or force closures, and as a result got 10% of the downloads the free version got, as opposed to Ghosttown with about 0.4%. I will never again use IAP for ad removal.

Situations where in-app billing makes sense

There may be a few non-game situations where IAP does make sense, however. For instance, if you want to sell plugins for an app but it makes no sense to sell them as separate apps because they do not work on their own. If you have a consistently used app and want to sell multiple premium upgrades, IAP could work for you. For instance, an app like Cardio Trainer with its multiple upgrade plugins might benefit from IAP.

In addition to plug-ins, you might consider using IAP as a back-up for pro version. Use both! Might as well give users a preference. Just make sure they know they are getting the same thing and that they don't mistakenly buy both.

The only other thing I can think of is if your app uses some sort of web service which charges per usage, like for instance a PDF-to-Fax app where you need to pay to send an electronic fax. If it's costing you say $0.50 per usage, you don't want one user using it 100 times and only paying $2.99 for the app, so you could instead charge for packs of 10 faxes. This protects you from your expenses ever exceeding your revenue.

Games are a different story!

Games are the perfect opportunity to up-sell premium features or components. When people get wrapped up or addicted to a game, they become very willing to pay for that better weapon or faster character to better their high scores. IAP is perfect for games, and if you are making a game on Android IAP is the only way to go.

GENIUS TIP: IAP IS THE PERFECT REVENUE MODEL FOR GAMES

In fact at the time of this writing 22 of the top 23 grossing Android games are free! If you are planning on creating a game for Android, use IAP. Period. Give away enough of the game for free that the user can become attached to the game and continually try to beat the high score, then allow IAP to get items which allow them to do bigger and better things to beat that score when they get stuck. Rare is the Android user who will pay for a game, but most people will be happy to pay $0.99 to relieve an hour of frustration trying to beat a high score.

6 PUBLICITY

It's kind of important

You've had a great idea, developed a stable, simple app, designed it well, priced it perfectly, and you are ready for launch. Now you just need to get the word out. Every step of the marketing process is important, and failure at one step can lead to failure of the entire app, but publicity may be the single most important part – it's certainly the part most people think of first when they think of marketing. You don't want to be the best kept secret on the Android Market – you want the launch of your app be a really big deal in the Android community. There are a lot of channels you need have in mind that you want to engage with your launch publicity marketing, such as Twitter, Facebook, blogs, directories, forums and everything else, but I've found that the best way to get the ball rolling is by getting featured on one of the big Android blogs. From there, many smaller sites will repackage their content, the big twitter accounts will take notice, and the big general software sites may even pick it up if it's a unique app. We'll get into the step by step process of making this happen in this chapter.

Breaking chicken/egg problem

Ah, the age old problem of app marketing. You sell a lot of apps by being ranked at the top of the app market listings, but you get ranked at the top of the app market listings by selling a lot of apps! How can we break this cycle and get enough sales at the outset to launch ourselves into one of those top spots? The only way people are going to find your app on launch day is by searching for it – there's simply no way they are going to stumble upon your app while browsing the market when it's got 0 downloads – your app won't be ranked high enough at that point. So how can you get people to specifically search for your app? Well, luckily the Android community is full of the type of people who follow blogs outlining new apps, and those people are just the type to want to try every new thing that comes out. You need to reach these "early adopters" and get them to search for your app in order to kick start the process of acquiring the download numbers you want and being to climb those rankings.

There is no disputing the best way to kick start your launch marketing – and that is by getting reviewed or featured by one of the big blogs in the Android community. I have personally had my 2 biggest recent apps (Media Converter and Ghosttown) reviewed by droid-life.com and android-central.com, 2 of the biggest android-specific blogs on the web. So how do you do it? Surely these websites gets tons and tons of email each day from people in search of free publicity. If you're going to get featured by one of these sites, you need to make a request, and it needs to stand out from the rest. Once you get one of them to accept, you can show that to their competitors and the rest of the blogs come much more easily.

Whether or not you can get that first blog to review your app is going to make or break your launch. Your review request email needs to stand out, and it needs to be done right. Writing this email is the single most important part of the launch marketing process, and that's why I've included an entire section to how to write it, and afterwards I've included a sample email:

Tips for requesting reviews on major Android blogs

- Find a specific writer for the blog who reviews apps and has reviewed a similar app on your site, and email him personally, rather than emailing the generic submission address
- Introduce yourself personally
- Be as clear as possible in your email subject. I used something like this: "Review Request –

MediaConverter for Android converts any file on your phone"

- Mention the writer by name in the beginning of the email
- Be frank that you are marketing your app and would like your app to be featured on the site
- The first sentence (after you've greeted the writer by name) should be used to explain exactly what makes your app unique.
- The entire email should be less than 5 sentences
- Include the following as attachments: the ad-free APK, 5 screenshots, high-res icon, and promotional graphic
- Pick one blog and email them days before launch, and mention that you are giving them the chance be the first to feature your app.
- Mention that you will share the blog post through your own marketing channels, giving the blog more page views.

Things NOT to do when requesting a review

- Tell them you have "the next big thing" or a "groundbreaking app" – nonsense phrases just waste time and make you seem less professional. Simply tell the writer what makes your app unique, and if it's impressive, they will be impressed.

- Require him to reply to you for the APK. Just attach it on the first email.
- Use a cryptic email subject like "Great app coming soon" – just mention that you are requesting a review in as few words as possible
- Email every writer at once. They'll find out and it will annoy them.

You have one goal when writing this email, and that is to convince the blogger that your app will provide something of value to their readers. They will post anything as long as their readers care about it, but they won't post anything that provides no value to their readers. Communicate this value as quickly as possible in your email, and keep it short.

Sample Request Email:

SUBJECT: Review Request: MediaConverter for Android converts any file on your phone

Hey Joe

My name is Jay Van Buiten and I am an Android Developer, and I wanted to give you a chance to have the first look at my new app which allows you to convert to and from virtually any file type right on your phone.

Media Converter is the only complete file conversion app for Android, giving you the power to convert to and from nearly any file format without having to connect to a computer.

I would appreciate if you could review this app on your blog. For your convenience, I've attached the APK, along with some screenshots, high-res icon, and promotional graphic.

Thanks,

Jay Van Buiten

No Success? Hire someone if you need to

If you've emailed all the major blogs and had no response, you may need to spend some cash if you still want to have a big launch. I've worked with a few mobile app marketing firms and I would recommend http://appsmarketing.mobi/. They have personal relationships with both droid-life.com and android-central.com and frequently get apps featured on those sites. While an email from you might get lost in the pile at a big site, a marketing firm is constantly communicating with these blogs and will always get an email response. Prices vary between firms, but you can expect to pay between $500-$1500 for a "launch package". I've paid for launch marketing twice, and both times I ended up making far more money because of the launch package than I spent.

Getting reviewed on a blog = $$$

In addition to kick starting your movement up the Android Market search rankings, you also get a nice taste of the kind of money you can make with a successful app. In my experience, when getting featured on a blog you can expect about 5-6x the amount of revenue you'd see on a normal good day. For instance, I make around $100 a day on Media Converter, and when I got featured on Droid-Life I made about $500 over the next 24 hours. You can see how paying around $1000 to a marketing firm to get featured on multiple blogs can pay for itself very quickly. I would recommend trying to contact blogs yourself first, especially if you don't have much of a budget, but paying for launch marketing is a smart backup option.

Other marketing channels

In addition to getting written about on blogs, there are obviously a number of other channels you need to be aware of, and take advantage of when trying generate publicity for your app. Let's take a look at each one of them, and I'll give you some tips I've learned from my own experience when launching my apps:

Twitter

Twitter is awesome. Maybe you even used their flexible and extensive API in your app. Twitter can be a powerful tool in spreading the word about your app. First of all, Twitter is a great way to get in contact with people who have a huge audience. I recommend using Twitter to introduce an app to blog writers through an @reply tweet, then mentioning your tweet in your subsequent email. This is just one more way to separate you from the competition in the blogs email box.

GENIUS TIP: USE TWITTER TO INITIATE RELATIONSHIP WITH BLOGGERS

You should make your twitter account at least a few days before launch, and start tweeting at bloggers about your upcoming app. Make sure your Twitter handle is simply your app name, and include the word android if the app is launching exclusively on Android. You can also start to generate some interest by using the search to look for people who are trying to solve the problem that your app solves. For instance, for my Media Converter app, I search twitter for "how to convert video Android" and found people asking how to convert videos directly on their phone. I simply tweeted at them and told them their problem would be solved in a couple days. When the app launches, give them the link, and the personal connection you've established will be a big help in convincing them to pay for your app. Remember, any app sales you can get on the first day of launch are much more valuable compared to the average sale, because it helps you break into that cycle of being ranked high and generating high downloads.

GENIUS TIP: A LAUNCH-DAY DOWNLOAD IS MORE VALUABLE THAN THE AVERAGE SALE, AS IT HELPS BREAK INTO THE HIGH-RANKING CYCLE AND INCREASES SALES FOR THE LIFTIME OF THE APP

Also make sure to use Twitter to retweet any posts or links about you. Use it to thank anyone who posts a blog about your app, and also reply to people who are wondering about, or have problems with your app.

Twitter search is also the best way to monitor your launch marketing progress! I'll go into more detail in the "monitoring progress" section coming up soon.

Facebook

Yep, Facebook is an important part of marketing for just about anyone, not just apps. Facebook is used in 2 very different ways depending on if your app is free or paid. For a free app, Facebook is a great way to spread the word about your app, as the social network lends itself to easy sharing and quick spreading of links and downloads. For a paid app, Facebook is important at launch to use your own network of friends to get those all-important launch-day downloads. As we've discussed, users are much less likely to share or tell their friends about a paid app since friends are much less likely to give it a try if they have to pay, so Facebook has less importance after launch for a paid app compared to a free app.

Either way, you should spend a few minutes setting up a Facebook page for your app around launch time and unashamedly ask your friends and family for "likes". This allows you to not only reach a few hundred of your own friends, but friends of friends will see when your friends "like" the page, so potentially thousands of people may hear about your app on launch day just from spending a few minutes on Facebook! The launch-day outreach you can do on Facebook can end up reaching as many people as a 2nd-tier blog review! This helps ensure a successful launch day, which again will help you ascend those rankings so you can start getting downloads from market "browsers" as opposed to just "searchers".

Blog Comments

While blog posts are extremely important and crucial to the launch process, they force you to depend on a writer to get your name on the blog. This can be risky and even in a best case scenario might take a few days, taking away from a potentially big launch day. But don't worry; there is another way to get thousands of blog readers to hear about your app, one that you can control all on your own – blog comments. I am not talking about spam! No one is going to download your app because you posted a link on a completely irrelevant blog post. But there will be blogs with articles that are relevant to your app, and if you can work the name of your app into the conversation, go for it! For instance, when I launched Ghosttown, it happened to be right around the time that Google was launching their cloud music service. This of course lead to a lot of blog posts on the subject of free streaming music, which means a lot of blog comments were discussing the top streaming services available. I politely mentioned Ghosttown on a few blogs, and some people said they tried it out! Also, having a link to your market listing on big-name sites, even if it's in a comment, will have a positive effect on that link's "relevance" according to Google, which can only help both your Google ranking and Android Market ranking.

YouTube

You should spend a few minutes making a demo video for your app – this doesn't have to be anything fancy, just make a quick, 1 minute video showing how your app works. This is a very valuable tool when emailing bloggers – it gives them a demo they can embed in the blog post and makes that post more valuable to the readers, and therefore more likely for the blogger to post. By giving bloggers all the promotional materials they need in an email attachment, you are making their job easier, and they will be more likely to help you out.

The Android Market also allows you to list a YouTube video within the app description to allow users to see a demo before purchasing. This is a very important tool to use, especially on a paid app when users may be wary of spending money on an app. Just make a quick demo video where to you demonstrate the main points of the app, and throw together a little title screen in Windows Movie Maker or iMovie, and it should be good enough. Users just want to know what they're getting before they give up the credit card number.

When to launch

This question is asked often, but there is no real good answer. In terms of when during the course of the year to launch – don't worry about that, you are better off launching when your app is ready rather than waiting extra time for a good launch period, it's not that important. But which day of the week you launch can affect your sales somewhat. I would recommend against launching on a weekend – people use their computer less and are less likely to be into the routine of checking their blogs and their Facebook and Twitter, etc. Launching on a Monday or Tuesday gives you 4-5 consistent days of high internet usage, and blogs are more likely to post on weekdays as well.

While your marketing effort and quality of marketing materials are the biggest contributors to launch success, it doesn't hurt to launch on the right day, so launch on a Monday or Tuesday unless other factors prevent that.

Monitoring progress

You'll want to keep a close eye on your progress during the launch days as far as which blogs are posting, how many tweets and Facebook shares you have, and obviously your sales. I would also recommend keeping a spreadsheet to track all your progress in one document, especially if you are working with someone to publicize the app or have a partner. Luckily, there are a lot of easy ways to track your progress:

Blog Posts

Blog posts can be tracked by 2 different methods: 1. A custom Google search alert. You can easily set up a search alert where Google will email you when new pages match your search query. It's not up to the minute, and it's kind of annoying because you'll get a lot of spam pages too. I would recommend my second method: 2. Twitter! Just about any blog will tweet when a new post goes up, so just search Twitter for the name of your app periodically and you'll be able to keep track of anywhere the app is talked about on the internet – except in private networks, such as Facebook.

Facebook

Tracking Facebook shares is really, really easy. Just add any URL (such as a blog post, or your actual market page) to the end of "http://graph.facebook.com/" and it tells you how many shares that URL has. For instance, to track how people shared the App of the Day post about my Ghosttown app on Droid-Life, I simply go to http://graph.facebook.com/http://www.droid-life.com/2011/05/26/app-of-the-day-ghosttown/, and bingo, I have 111 shares.

7 ADVERTISING

Pay to get paid

Is it worth it?

Paying to advertise your app on mobile devices rarely makes financial sense. If you are like most independent app developers, and have a small marketing budget (or no budget at all), you can get by without paying for advertising. The simple fact is that it almost always will cost more to acquire each new user than you will make from that user. If you have a large budget and a long-term outlook, and are willing to take a loss in the initial launch period in order to gain more market share, then you should look into advertising your app. Since this book is written from the perspective of a low-budget independent developer, and is mostly written for low-budget independent developers, we are going to look at forms of advertising that makes sense in those situations. These are ways to advertise without paying out of pocket, or by at least guaranteeing you make more money then you are spending.

Admob

If you have a free app and are monetizing it through ads, Admob (the leading advertiser for Android, recently bought out by Google) gives you the option to convert that money directly into advertising credits, so you can test out how effective advertising can be for your app, without having to pay money out of pocket. Committing to recycling your ad revenue into advertising credits for, say, your first month can be a good way to boost downloads during your launch periods and evaluate the effectiveness of advertising. If you think you are at a point where you make more off the advertising than you spend, keep it going!

Mdotm

Mdotm is one of the few advertisers that allow you to guarantee that you won't lose money on an advertising experiment. How Mdotm works is that you literally pay for installs. If you don't get any downloads, you don't pay. You simply state what you are willing to bid on each download, so if you're app cost $2.99 (and you make 70% of that on every sale), you may consider bidding $0.99 for each download. If you don't get any downloads, you pay nothing, and if you do get downloads, you are obviously guaranteed to make money on each one. Of course, this doesn't work for free apps.

Advertise on your own free apps

This is a marketing tactic which has made me a lot of money but is rarely discussed in other Marketing guides. You can make money on paid apps which might otherwise not get a lot of visibility on the Market by using your free (and highly downloaded) apps to advertise them. I used this strategy myself with 2 apps: Ghosttown and Number Spy. Ghosttown was free and was a very popular app since it provided a lot of unique value and was free without any restrictions. NumberSpy was a good Caller ID app, but had a hard time differentiating from other Caller ID apps and could not get near the top of the rankings for any high-volume searches. Instead of paying for advertising for NumberSpy, which may have cut my profitability even further, I simply took advantage of the high usage my free app was getting and put an ad from NumberSpy on the first activity for every Ghosttown user. Sales from Number Spy went from less than $10 a day to around $50 a day.

You can even elect to split ads between ads for your own apps and regular ad network ads- this way you can compare which option makes more money for you, and switch that method permanently once you've decided that you've gathered enough data to make the decision.

Contact a developer and work out an agreement

One last advertising option for low-budget developers is to work around ad networks by working out an agreement with other developers. You can either advertise for free on each other's apps, or do a one-way transaction where you pay a set price per month. For instance, if you have a very niche app, let's say a tool for developers to keep track of downloads, advertising on a general ad network would waste a lot of money since 99% of people viewing the ads would have no use for the program. It would be a better idea to contact a developer of another app in the same niche and advertise your app to the specific audience you are targeting.

GENIUS TIP: YOU WASTE MONEY BY ADVERTISING OUTSIDE OF YOUR NICHE

8 MONETIZATION

Finally

Money! You make apps to make money, hopefully quite a bit of money. Most of the marketing strategy discussed so far in the book has been aimed at getting as many downloads as possible. Downloads are great, but you don't pay for a mortgage in downloads. You need to be able to convert those downloads into cash. You can have a great marketing strategy but without a good monetization strategy, you won't make nearly as much money as you could. Obviously, monetization strategy matters a lot more when talking about free apps, as there is a very strong correlation between paid downloads and cash (although there is an exception! And we will deal with that in the last part of this chapter). Everyone knows of the 2 biggest monetization strategies: paid downloads and advertising, but they are a number of ways to convert downloads into cash, and you need to decide which one will be most effective in your situation if you want to make as much money as possible. We have covered paid downloads and in-app purchases extensively in the pricing chapter (go back if you didn't read it!), so this section will be about monetizing ads through other means.

Advertising

If you have a free app, you have a few options for monetization: Sell additional features via in-app purchases, which we've talked about in the pricing section, sell a separate pro version, which we've also discussed in detail, or keep the app completely free, and make money on ad space. Obviously these aren't the only ways to make money on free apps, but these are by far the 3 most well-traveled paths. While we've already covered IAP and pro versions, it's time to go into detail about how to monetize your app effectively using ads.

Choosing an ad network

How do you choose exactly which ad network to use in your app? There is basically one crucial consideration: Which will pay you the most eCPM (ie. How much will you be paid per ad view?). There are 2 basic choices for Android developers: AdMob and Mobclix. European developers should also look into MobFox – here's the pros and cons of each.

AdMob

Admob has recently been bought out by Google and is the king of ads in the Android realm. AdMob pays well for most users, as my research indicates you can expect somewhere in the ballpark of $0.50 eCPM (Obviously this number can vary wildly depending on your app). This means for every 1000 ads you show, you make $0.50. It doesn't seem like a lot, but with good marketing, if you can get a few hundred thousand downloads and a fair percent of your users using your app, you can get into the tens of thousands of dollars per year pretty quickly, and a hit app with over a million downloads and high usage can get you $100,000 a year. On the other hand, a "tool" app that only gets used once in a while and isn't targeted towards a large audience is not going to make much money. But we've been over this in the "Pricing" chapter, so I'll assume if you've chosen to release a free app you've made the right decision.

Admob gives up-to-the minute reporting and allows you to choose which type of demographic uses your app so you can show more targeted ads, which are more likely to be clicked. Because AdMob is owned by Google, you'll never need to worry about the company going out of business (if Google goes out of business we'll all have bigger problems than our ad network!), or not getting paid on time. In my experience with AdMob, you'll get your check on time every month, and there are never any issues with the online reporting not matching the check. But that's how you'd expect it to be, right? Well, not if you've ever worked with MobClix.

MobClix

MobClix is not actually an ad network. What MobClix does is automatically signs you up for just about every mobile ad network (except AdMob), and bids those networks against each other each time a user view an ad. As you would expect, revenues on MobClix far exceed any individual ad network (I've seen my eCPM approaching $1.00, and other users have reported up to $5 per 1000 views!). MobClix is great, until you actually want your cash.

MobClix is notorious for not paying on time, and you can confirm this with a quick Google search of their name – the results are full of people complaining about never being paid. MobClix, like AdMob was recently bought out by a company named Velti which was supposed to help their financial problems. They just moved to a new system where they promise to pay you the full amount you are owed 90 days after the month you earned the revenue (it sucks, but it's actually better than the old system of basically paying you when they had the money). Still, I am currently writing this on day 106 and haven't received any money for the month I should have been paid for already. If you complain enough, email enough people, and warn people in public forums never to use MobClix, you'll get paid eventually – but it's annoying. MobClix also has issues with changing the amount you made on ads days after the fact! MobClix's reliability issues are in stark contrast to Admob's stability, but the additional revenue may make it worth the risk.

Only sign up for MobClix with the understanding you won't see your money for a long time, and you'll have to eventually make a scene in order to get it.

MobFox

MobFox is a new ad network targeted toward European developers. If you are located in Europe, and your target audience is European, give it a shot, because many developers have reported very high number with MobFox. I tried, but got very low revenue – but I'm in the U.S.

Try Everything!

When starting out, simply allocate a certain percentage of traffic to each network you want to try out. Once you feel like you've gathered enough data to make a decision, switch most of your traffic that network. Some networks even allow you to send traffic to another ad network if the bid for that ad doesn't reach a certain amount. Try different combinations and see what works for you!

Choosing types of ads

There are ads, and there are annoying ads. Annoying ads make more money in the short term, but piss off users. There are basically 3 types of ads – banner ads (the ones you see on most free apps), full page ads (covers the full screen, usually requires a button press to get past it), and video ads (15 or 30 seconds ads which cover the whole screen, requiring you to either wait or possibly presenting a "skip" option). I would recommend only using banner ads, unless you have a specific scenario where either a full screen ad or a video ad is a good fit. For instance, there is precedent for playing videos ads before premium video content, such as on Hulu. Also, if the user needs to wait for something to happen anyway, such as waiting for a file to process or something to download before they can do anything else, that would be a good opportunity to show a video ad. Full page ads are also a good idea when you are waiting for something to load that usually takes a long time, especially in a situation where you have nothing else to present besides the "loading" dialog.

A good rule of thumb for when to use the larger, more annoying ads, is whether you've seen them in that situation before on successful apps. For instance, no user is going to tolerate watching a 30 second video before they can even use the app, but a user would probably be willing to sit through a 15-second video before watching 30 minutes of premium content. The easiest thing to do is to just stick to banner ads, or only use large ads in situations where the user would need to sit and wait anyway.

Remember that the more intrusive your ads are, the less enjoyable your user experience will be. Lower user satisfaction means lower retention rates, lower usage, and lower Market ratings, which ultimately means fewer downloads and less money in your pocket. Don't place ads in every empty space you can find just to get your eCPM up by 1 or 2 cents. You are always better off keeping the ads reasonable and building your user base by making an app that is enjoyable to use and marketing it well.

Remove ads with in-app billing

It can't hurt to give users the choice to use in-app billing to remove ads. You will almost never make 99 cents from an individual user viewing ads, no matter how often he uses the app, so it's never a bad idea to give users the choice to remove ads in the app for 99 cents.

I've used this method myself in my Ghosttown app, and was pretty surprised at how few users removed the ads. In fact, only about 1 in every 300 users elected to remove the ads! It still didn't hurt as it was all money that I otherwise would not have made, but don't base your entire revenue model on this strategy. It's a nice bonus and there's no reason not to do it (unless you have a pro version where being ad-free is one on the features), so go ahead and throw it in.

Pro versions

If you have a paid app, you should release a free demo if possible to get people to try before you buy – but that's not what I mean when I say "pro" version. As opposed to a paid app with a free demo, in this scenario the free app is the one you are marketing, and the paid version is for more advanced users who want to add features. The free app does everything the app is supposed to do, and the paid app takes it to the next level. You still have all the marketing benefits of a free app, while giving yourself another angle to make money.

I would urge anyone in this situation to be careful not to exclude useful features from the free version just to make the pro version more valuable. This will hurt your ability to market the free version, and less people will be aware of your pro version as a result. Instead, only use a pro version as revenue tool if there are specific features that only certain, more advanced users would be interested in, and be willing to pay for.

Generic paid apps

An unorthodox way of making money on a free app is to make a generic paid app and advertise it on the free app. We've talked about using your paid apps in tandem with your free apps to make more total revenue, but this takes it a step further. You make a generic, easy to make app in a crowded niche for the sole purpose of advertising it on your free app. The paid app should be in a category where most people aren't aware of free alternatives without doing research (for instance, people know they can get wallpapers for free, but maybe they don't know they can get a ringtone maker for free). A great thing to do for this is to just tweak an open source app and advertise it on your free app for $1.99 or so. It's an interesting experiment and you just might find out that you make more money using this tactic than with regular ads.

Other marketplaces

In addition to the Android Market, you can add a little revenue to the pile by publishing your app in other markets as well. The 2 biggest ones are of course the Amazon App Store, and GetJar.

Amazon

At the time of this writing, the Amazon app store won't make you a lot of revenue. People seem to simply use it to get the free app of the day every day, and then use the more familiar Android Market for everything else – but that is all set to change with the release of the Amazon Kindle Fire. It won't hurt to be one of the first to jump on this train and make kindle specific versions of your apps made for the 7" screen. Unfortunately, the Fire does not run Honeycomb so you can't simply re-release other tablet apps.

You should release all of your apps on Amazon just to cover all your bases, but be aware of Amazon's strange terms of service: You aren't allowed to remove your own apps, and you are obligated to leave them on the Amazon store as long as they are on the Android Market. In addition, Amazon can change your price without your permission, and even make it the free app of the day. – meaning people that may have paid for your app eventually on the Android market will already have it for free because they saw it on Amazon. If you are aware of, and OK with these terms, go ahead and increase your app's exposure by releasing on the Amazon app store.

GENIUS TIP: AMAZON'S APP STORE HAS A RIDICULOUS TERMS OF SERVICE AGREEMENT, BE AWARE OF IT BEFORE YOU UPLOAD YOUR APPS!

GetJar

GetJar is set to release GetJar Gold, a program service which gives users unlimited paid apps for free – in return for having to view sponsored listings within the "store". I am wary of trying this because while GetJar pays you for every download, you won't get as much as you get in the Android Market, so it's really just the same user-base downloading your apps at lower prices. You may want to check this out for yourself, though.

Avoid piracy

Why does the number of users of your paid apps not always correlate directly to revenue? Because some people are using your app without paying for it! On any paid app you publish, make sure to include the Android Licensing Library. It takes about 40 minutes to implement the first time, and about 5 minutes for every app after that – so it's no big deal. Of course, everything can be cracked, so it's an even better idea to put a remote kill switch in your app – just put a quick check to a webpage on your own hosting that runs in a seperate thread. If the webpage instructs the app to close, it should close. This allows you remotely disable certain versions of your app so your app can never be permanently cracked – you can always fix the vulnerability and issue an update. This is especially useful if you are paying for a service that runs within your app such as an API – while you might not make money off pirates either way, you certainly don't want them *costing* you money!

GENIUS TIP: IF YOUR EXPENSES ARE LINKED TO APP USAGE, MAKE SURE YOU CAN REMOTELY DISABLE PIRATED APPS IF NESSECARY

9 MARKET VISIBILITY

Should be 20/20

OK, so you've come up with a great idea, designed the app well, picked a great title, icon and description, you've priced it perfectly, and you have your launch strategy and blog emails ready to go. While all these things are of extreme importance in marketing your app, the single greatest factor in sustainable app success is making sure your app ranks highly in the Android Market – whether that's ranking highly for the search terms you have targeted, or ranking highly in your category in general. The more times people see your app as an option in the Market, the more downloads you'll get. If you've done a great job on the rest of your marketing techniques, you should have an app listing that will convince people to buy your app when they see it. Now you just need to make sure they see it – so in addition to getting high download numbers, here are some more tips for how to increase the amount of users that will see your app in the Market.

Get listed in multiple categories

Yes, it's possible! In addition to being listed in your regular category (ie. Tools, Media, etc), you can also easily get yourself listed in the Live Wallpaper and

Widgets categories by simply having those things in your app. Obviously some apps would have no reason to have a live wallpaper, but for most apps you can figure out a reason to throw a widget in there. Spending a day or two developing a live wallpaper and/or widget will almost certainly benefit you in the long run, as you may be stumbled upon by anyone browsing those 2 categories, in addition to your usual category.

Only use needed permissions

People love freaking out about permissions. The average user doesn't understand what they do, but they know it helps you access their information, which they don't like. Scroll through the reviews of just about any app, and you'll find people complaining about the permissions and coming up with conspiracy theories about apps stealing their information. In addition, Google doesn't like you using too many permissions either – that's why they have them in the first place instead of giving you access to all of them by default. Using unnecessary permissions can hurt your ranking – make sure before you publish that you don't give yourself access to any permissions that you don't need to use.

The most common example of this is using location data solely to deliver ads. You should run some tests first and find out if you even make more money on ads by doing that. If not, scrap it.

Different languages

Android allows you use to use localization to load different sets of text and graphics for different languages. Supporting different languages will obviously increase your downloads in foreign countries, but it also helps your Market ranking. Even making a few xml files for the most common foreign countries using Google Translate can't hurt, especially if your app has a lot of text or instructions.

Keywords

Keywords! No, this isn't 1999 where you write "Britney Spears" 1000 times at the bottom of your page to get to the top of the search results, but keywords are still important. Obviously, you want to make sure to include the search terms you are targeting somewhere in your description, but you can also use your description text to make sure you appear for a variety of other searches. For instance, you may want to mention the name of your competitor and describe the features you have that they don't – not just to convince people to buy your app instead of theirs, but so when someone searches for that other app, you'll come up in the search as well. If you have a nicer looking icon and a clearer title (which you should if you've read this book), then maybe they'll check out your app as well. You can also use your description to mention current events or trends – let's say you have an app that lets you keep track of TV shows. You may want to mention the latest hit TV show because it will probably have a lot of new fans and therefore be generating a lot of searches.

Remember to keep these search terms within the text of the description, not just written out in succession at the bottom. Google is smart and those keywords won't have nearly as much value as those placed in sentences with other important words.

Remember, if someone in your target audience is searching, you want to make sure they find you. Use your description to make that happen.

Acceleration/Velocity

Acceleration is the name of the game! If your app is getting more and more downloads each day, you'll be "trending" and start to climb the rankings very quickly (not to mention appearing on the actual new "trending" category). This why a strong launch is so important. Slow growth is nice, but if you can have 3 consecutive days where the app really explodes, you will climb the rankings very quickly and break into that beautiful cycle of high rankings and high downloads. But it works the other way as well – if you start to have less and less downloads each day, your app will begin to fall. This is where velocity comes in – you need to break into those high rankings (let's say Top 50 in your category) in order to pick up the "browsers" and not just the "searches". These extra downloads from browsers will allow you to maintain consistency and not fall even farther out of the top rankings. This will buy you time to appear on that next big blog, and send your ranking even higher.

Great reviews

Reviews are absolutely huge when it comes to rankings. That extra half star can be the difference between top 100 and top 20. This is why it's so important to keep an eye on reviews – especially in the first few days. During your first week, you should just leave the tab open on your developer console and be monitoring reviews by the minute. When someone mentions a force close or a large issue or something you can fix – drop what you are doing and fix it, issue an update, and send that user an email to tell them it's fixed. This will prevent future complaints about the same thing and maybe even get that person to change their reviews.

4 stars should be the standard, as there are so many different devices and form factors that your app is bound to have some small issues, but getting to 4.5 or 5 stars can really set your app apart and take your Market ranking to the next level.

Use new API features

Google loves when you use their new features and APIs. For instance, having an app that uses NFC and location and live wallpapers and widgets and in-app purchases and licensing will rank much higher than an app that uses none of these. Of course, you shouldn't put unnecessary features in your app just for a slightly higher ranking, but think of it as a bonus reason to include these features in the first place, if they make sense for your particular app.

Active user rate

This is a big one. There are two ways that Google can read how well existing customers enjoy the app – one is reviews, and the other is active user rate. This is the amount of users that still have the app installed on their device, compared to the amount of total downloads. This number has a huge impact on your Market ranking. It's probably too late to change how useful your app is for users an ongoing basis, for instance some apps are just naturally the kind of app that is used on a regular basis while others, such as my file converter app, may be just be a one-time use. But I've found that one thing that has an incredibly high effect on active user rate, and that's your icon. When users go through their app drawer uninstalling apps they no longer want, they will be a lot more likely to uninstall an app that makes their phone look ugly than one that looks really cool. A good active user rate is 75%. In the past, most of my apps have been in the 50-60% range, but for the past few apps I've done, I decided to use generic, really colorful, cool looking icons as opposed to trying to make an icon that accurately portrayed what the app did. My active user rate for Media Converter is above 90%! Now, I can't prove that the icon has been responsible for all of this change, but it certainly helps. Just another reason to have a beautiful icon!

10 MAINTENANCE

Almost done

Congrats. Your app is out. It had a great launch. It's selling well due to your genius marketing plan. You are rich, or at least making some money. But your work is not done! They are still some daily tasks you need to stay on top of to insure that your app stays near the top of the rankings and sales don't start to slip.

Respond to users

Users love when you respond to emails immediately. I'm going to make the wild assumption that you own a smartphone so you don't even have to check your email. When you get that email notification and it's from a customer, just reply immediately. Tell them you'll look into it soon, or even look at their order really quick and help them out right away. A customer that feels like they are getting great service is more likely to return the favor by giving you a great review. On the other hand, leaving customers waiting or forgetting to reply to them means they may leave a bad review or feel like they are getting scammed, and you don't want that.

Give refunds

Just give refunds to people when they ask. It's not worth the 2 or 3 bucks or whatever it is to be arguing with customers and upsetting them, leading to even more bad reviews. Think of it this way – while you may be losing 2 dollars, you would probably lose even more from lost customers due to a bad, angry review being at the top of your description page. Personally, I use this as a selling point. I say in all my descriptions that I am happy to give refunds at any time for any reason – this encourages people to download the app and not feel like their money is at risk. If you are worried about people abusing this system and using your app and then just getting their money back anyways, I can at least tell you that I lose less than $10 on refunds for every $1000 I make. Happy customers make you money, angry ones make you lose money.

Frequent updates

Update your app! Keep a constant eye on your reviews and your bug reports, and if there's a problem with your app, drop what you are doing and fix it. Issue the update immediately. Not only will this keep bad reviews to a minimum, but you'll also show up on the "Just In" category for users with the old version of the market (the new one doesn't have this category anymore). Frequently updated apps also get a higher market ranking than those which are uploaded and not cared for.

That's it!

You've made it through the journey of developing and marketing a successful Android app. If you have any questions, comments, or tips I didn't think of, I'd love to hear from you:

GeniusAndroidMarketing@gmail.com

Tweet me @GeniusAndroid